Minutiae

Title: Minutiae / Kirsten Johnston
ISBN 9780645797718

Cover image: Kirsten Johnston
Image title: 'When it Rains'
(acrylic on canvas, 100 x 200cm: 2023)

Publisher: Walleah Press
South Launceston
Tasmania, Australia 7249
www.walleahpress.com.au
ralph.wessman@walleahpress.com.au

Minutiae

Kirsten Johnston

CONTENTS

I. Home

II. Visiting Hours

III. Unfurling

IV. Road Trip

V. Too Much Time

VI. Art Should

1. Home

Going home from Robe

My shadow precedes me
when the asphalt tends eastward.
It announces my coming until the road swings south
and a companion travels by my side.
The sky lifts away.
Late-day chill sidles in to subdue the land.
The earth steels itself for a frost tonight.

The road scrolls under me, is spat out behind,
lies chastened and reversed in the rear-view mirror.
Scrubby trees born of this sandy soil huddle
in the sea air; salty, stinging, icy in the evening.
Ewes and offspring shelter on the leeward side—
winter lambing has its perils. The roadside underlay
of rank clumps of dead kikuyu is darkening green.
The grazed land beyond the fences is manicured—
feeding stock keep the pasture sweet.

Closer to home, the pine plantations murmur
their mysteries and cast a premature night.
I watch for roos. This is their country.
My headlights ignite reflectors. I follow the red.

Autumn progeny

New lambs, knobble-kneed
and wrinkled like elbows,
teeter in the sun, warming as cats
before breeze blows the day away.
In random sequence, they jerk legs
flared with woolly cuffs to chase milk.
Tired mothers feed on pasture
already into its winter-waning
but juicy green like paint.
Lambs fluoresce against the grass,
shining like healed skin,
not yet dirty-dull like the mob.
The crows shine too, with pupils
black and deep as wells.
They perch on wires, or pick
at soft ground among the flock,
waiting for dead or close enough.

September Canola Crop

Eucalypts wade hip-deep in gold.
Spindly-legged hay sheds stand on tiptoes,
take refuge on islands sinking into the sulphur sea.

I long to swim in the yellow, immerse myself,
tumble in its waves, float on its effervescent froth
dancing in wind-ripples.

Canola is draped to the horizon
in folds, swathes, arm-waving gestures.
It feeds on its own glory—confident, bold.
Sassy. I am bewitched.

Sister crops—dusty beans, lucerne,
wheat in English green—sway unseen,
invisible in the glare of September.

By October, brilliance fades, gold will lean to brown.
Warmth ripens black seeds born of flowers—
idealism bowing to destiny, the purpose of existence.
By November: twigs and spikes,
pods and stems crisp like baked skin.
In December: stripped of treasure, discarded.

But September's crop knows none of this.
It wallows in celebrity and camera flashes.
It ingests the heady drug of renown.
Canola lives close to the edge.

Vintage

Coonawarra, South Australia

Stella serves night shift in the winery,
wrangling hoses like elephant trunks,
moving juice from vessel to vessel,
pumping wine over floating skins.
It's heavy work. The blunt smell of fermentation
sticks to her clothing. She counts the minutes and the dollars,
toting up progress towards that car.
Machinery noise sneaks under her earmuffs:
motors and clanging metal on metal.
There's nothing romantic about vintage.

It's not just Stella. Coonawarra
is consumed by the collection of grapes
hanging rich and ripe from fading vines.
From the bite of early morning through weary night
lights and colours flirt in the vineyards.
Tractors drag tall bins to receive
streams of tumbling gifts spewed from conveyors.
Once harvesters have prowled,
great sucking, shaking monsters,
the rows are shabby with tousled hair.

Vintage is a collective adventure.
Like an ensemble cast, there is a role for all—
stars, extras, editors, dogsbodies.
A community unites.

It seems endless, like the volume of liquid
gushing through Stella's hands. But the vines
have only so much to give. With the last vat sealed,
the last silver tanker dispatched, the last hose flushed,
a sigh is felt to the horizon, a tired smile shared
between colleagues and, for Stella at least,
a long, cold beer taken in celebration.

Scrabbling at 'The Grape'

The Sweet Grape Café, Penola, South Australia

The way they look at us
you'd think Sue and I
were raving eccentrics wearing layers
of Indian skirts and funny hats.
We unpack the Scrabble
and angle the board, leaving room
for the iced chocolate and long black
we order from the girl with uncertain eyes.
(Are games *allowed* in cafés?)
We agree, in deference to a stunned public,
to play demurely
and restrict our abuses to whispers:
'Q on a triple letter! You cow!'
When lunch is delivered, my soup goes cold
and Sue's beef roll dries at the fringe
as she battles with no vowels at all
and I must dispose of
A A A E I I R.

I should have stopped

Early morning. The eastern sky still black.
I hadn't seen roos. I was watching.
Silver fence-lines ran backwards in the headlights,
shadows shifted as I passed. I maintained my speed.
A long way to go.

Around a bend,
the yellow dog turned his head towards me
eyes hollow-empty in the bright.
Brakes. Instinct.
The black shape he stood over didn't move.
Headlights barely picked him out from the asphalt.
Two dogs: one dead, one loyal.

I gave them wide berth.
I should have stopped.

A long way to go.

Metro café

Mount Gambier, South Australia

I feel the warmth as I lower myself into café comfort.
They know me here. That is worth the five dollars fifty,
even before I get my coffee.
Mark greets me as he does most Sundays,
writes my order on the slip like a mind reader.

The coffee is gentle, soft. Hannah has made it today.
Sometimes she talks to me about her kids
and she came to an exhibition of mine once.
I relax into the baked bread smell.
My edges blur like the artwork in the crèma.

A crack of laughter bolts from the kitchen—
an honest eight in the morning guffaw,
the best way to start a shift.
One day I will stay till closing, immerse myself,
wash away time and sit with a book
or wine or a piece of that carrot cake.

Today I must rouse myself, however,
not because the coffee has gone cold
but because the lesser things of life
bleat like lost lambs.
I'll be back at opening tomorrow
for more than I pay for.

II. Visiting Hours

Visiting hours

Her mood is brittle like old bakelite—
one wrong word spawns tears
or rage or bitter silence like death.
Age has rotted away her filters—
she says more than she thinks,
demands more than she needs.

I visit once a fortnight which she says she loves
in a voice with sad edges because no-one else comes,
but the time leaves us both stretched and pummelled,
pulled through a wringer like the one she mourns,
reliving her own roaring twenties in the face of mine.
I am battered from dodging feelings

but a grandmother is important,
a link to a time swiftly lost,
and a person of dignity, mostly.
Even among the turmoil of chaotic emotional minions,
a mind is still grimly holding court.
She is a fading monarch,
slipping in and out of the throne
like a foot in worn house slippers
but as snappy as an argument,
like patience at the end of its tether.

There's that man

There's the man with broken spirit,
traipsing with head so long bent,
spine so curled, he can't look forward,
a breaking wave of a body.
He follows familiar paths like the blind
or sad, eyes and soul fixed to ground
that refuses to swallow him,
treading in what isn't,
stepping on dreams he can't remember.

Sunflowers

after 'Sunflowers' by Vincent van Gogh

She gathered the sunflowers for him
early, when the dew on grass broomsticks still swept her legs,
and took her time to arrange their yellow heads to face all around.
Their excitement prickled on their petals
and their dark, anticipating eyes reflected light from the window.

But even as she watched them
they lost their moist smiles,
became jaded and delivered less of what they'd promised.
The light also faded and the afternoon
couldn't hold back evening any longer.

She waited for him to come, to leave
the large, black-haired wife he'd said was a burden to him,
and arrive with his soft hands and a bottle of Chianti
to stretch the day into tomorrow, into the rest of her life.
The flowers, deprived of sun,
drooped despite the brightness of her candles
and the crystals of sugar, laced with tears,
she dropped into their water.

Old Man, Old Dog

Mount Gambier, South Australia

The old man walks in jerks,
age has swept away fluidity
and left bones dry and stiff,
an empty river.
Bowed legs make shuffling progress
past the gallery building, feet tired
but determined.

Behind him, the yellow-cream Labrador,
back broad, round haunches,
white-muzzled by years,
treads the same gait—
stuttering, rocking, a child's robot.

Joined by a string they disappear
down steps behind the Town Hall,
old man in front, dog lagging
having more weary legs to move.
The slow, unison clump-clack, clump-clack,
of shoes and claws on metal stairs
echoes across the gardens
and merges with the hushing of the waterfall.

Dad's Golf Clubs

Dusty now, black leather bag, soft from years,
heavy like grief. Wide pockets cluttered—
balls, some with old Melbourne dirt still nestled in dimples,
some new-branded white, never used, bought too late;
tees, whole and broken; old scorecards,
his name at the top in back-slanted writing,
reluctantly turned in when the numbers were too high.
The hood, to keep the Kingston Heath rain out, is floppy now,
a petal unfurling to reveal its stamens—
silver club heads, treasured, effective even in his seventies.
The nectar is memories of lessons, hitting with him.

This is a bag deep enough for love,
melancholy,
and wishing.

Old Merv

Spittle-mouthed and toothless
he grabs me as I leave the pub.
His grasping hands,
bones breaking through paper skin,
fingers missing,
curl around my coat, drag at it,
forcing me to swing around and see him.
Crooked, filthy face,
white hair, erect with fright at itself,
eyes that wash blankly over me.
Eyes that tell nothing and everything about him.
The gravel-scrape of his voice scratches in my ears:
Spare enough for a beer, missy?
I brush him away like a spider
with a shudder born of fear.
Missy?
but I've gone.

Roger the Extra

He is mute, a figurant,
one of the masses that rabbles on
while actors shine.
He gasps, arrives, looks on.
This week a doorman, a shopper,
a soldier. Making a living not living.

Roger is impassive in the wings,
waits to faint, sigh, scurry, fossick,
slump in the courtroom, read in the café,
cry out when the hero tumbles
from a chipboard balcony.

Easy money, a walk
in a cardboard-and-poster-paint park.
A paper doll, dumb.
After the show, hair still awry,
he trudges home
yelling dialogue of the leads to the listening stars.

My Mother's Hands

My mother's hands are a soft voice singing and a finger tickling my palm: *Round and Round the Garden*. More able than she will ever know, my mother's hands have defeated monsters and created people. They have held the lightness of babies, soothed crying dogs, gripped slippery chicken breasts to chop. Her nails, although cut short, have brought the garden inside until it was washed away with the suds of muddy sports clothes.

Their skin is fragile. She wears gloves to weed.

My mother's hands have polished tables to a high, hard shine. They have smacked in discipline; just once. Strong in youth, they could open any jar, jam the spiky handles into the hard ends of corn cobs, grip mine to cross the road.

They prickle with arthritis but never give in. They are stoic.

My mother's hands have stroked my wakeful back. They have cradled books, arranged sprigs of eucalypt and levered her under the house to fix the heating ducts. They have manipulated the tiny seeds of plants and raked the leaves of their mature cousins.

Her wedding ring can't be removed; her knuckles are swollen.

My mother's hands have glued models, picked up the dropped stitches in my knitting, solved maths and played Bach. They have wrinkled in the dishwater and rested on the hot sand of Cottesloe beach. They have folded tents, rubbed sunscreen, guided us through childhood and applauded our adult years.

I hold them now.

III. Unfurling

Winter

Winter breath snuffs candles.
Light is a failing companion
in a greyed world
where ends of days take cover.

This ice-scented season prickles my nose,
makes real misty exhalations
as my body clashes with a
determined world.

I bend around my chest to keep out
air that is solid and sharp like metal,
that makes me jerky, stiffens me,
bites my nervous skin.

The washed world has crisp edges.
Colours deepen,
roads wetted to black take on
a blinding shine in the morning.

In my monochrome garden,
the thirst of summer quenched,
holly berries glow red—
a reminder that winter is an adventure.

I step out in a scarlet coat.

Quiet Dawn

Blush, that sky
coy about coming to town
dressed in her best.
Not like her sister in brilliant golds
or the pinks that give warning,
she is demure, with light
on her sheer skirts,
twirling into day, elegant
like a fine rosé is smooth.
Up early and gone, she leaves an echo
we can barely see.

Cold

The cold curls around my legs like a needy cat,
its tendrils caressing my calves.
I move it away with my feet but it is persistent.

The cold is an opportunist
seizing every chance to introduce itself.
It longs to be my lover. It rubs my back,
holds my hands, flicks up my shins where the trousers hang away.

The cold wants to wrap me up and comfort me.
Like my mother, it takes me in its arms,
holding me as if there is
a lifetime of sadness to cure.

Grevillea flowering

Curled like toes, twisted,
still wrapped in themselves,
they grow and colour,
these hidden tendrils of spring.

Days lengthen and bring the slow motion
flick from the buds, falling like arms from covers
on a languid morning.

Reds, pinks, even golds unfurl in succession,
each elegant calligraphy finished with an ink blot.
Spidery forms creep over forbidding foliage
and suck the sun.

Rain

Rain falls lightly,
unsure like Grandma's tap at the door;
gains confidence with the wind
and strengthens,
making a statement, 'I am here,'
like Grandpa sitting down for the roast;
slides into arrogance,
settles in like Uncle Mac
in front of the footy,
and stays all afternoon.

August Morning

The air is hard.
Frost makes white the breath of early walkers,
brisk like brooms, hands curled.
The earth wakes to an ice-clear self,
loud with colour and sharp edges,
an abstract painting.
A bold sky makes promises about sun
but still sucks yesterday's warmth
like a sponge.
Growing large out of frozen feet,
day claims its place.

IV. Road Trip

The Hay Plains

New South Wales
(the flattest place in the Southern Hemisphere)

Sydney. Five hundred and thirty miles to go.
Around a corner, a sudden realisation away,
the ground drops its shoulders,
falls to the floor.

The land is taut, stretched like lycra
pulled over a table, pinned with scrub.
Saltbush punctures the fabric—shallow-rooted and silver,
it repeats into a misty distance.

Trees, trunks like upward fingers, struggle for breath,
stunted and flat like the terrain they find little
in a black-grey clay, one day to be liberated by wind,
carried as dust to the Great Divide.

The road tips forward, asphalt carpet
slipping over the sunken horizon
into the dawn's sky-haze of forever blue.

It is openness that smells of freedom.

                    It is freedom that tastes like flying.

Morning at Rydges Hotel

Adelaide

It's well before dawn. A growl
of early traffic on Anzac Parade
rises to the sixth floor like smoke,
seeps through the balcony windows and settles
on bed sheets dishevelled by insomnia.
When I drag apart tall curtains to watch the contrails,
whites and reds bubbling in rivers,
the cold through the glass is an affront.

The dark feels like forever,
though the sky has relinquished its deepest ink.
It waits for light: patient, confident
like those who know they're loved.

My eyes are scratchy from lack of sleep—
it hasn't come, that misbehaving dog.
The hands on my watch creep
as they have since three
and tell me it's too late now.

I long for coffee, a thick latte
to comfort the night away,
but I must wait like the shadows.
No one hides behind hissing machines at this hour,
and I have picked the mini bar dry.

Bullarto South

Central Victoria

The land slopes to the dam inviting us
to roll like coins around and around
and down to the muddy edge.

There is water now.
Not like '98
when its inner skin was exposed,
cracked deep and hard.
We scratched the jagged blocks,
stabbed long sticks in the gaps.

March grass is lumpy with tussocks,
a carpet laid by careless tradesmen
over discarded toys. Maples,
chimney-tall, own their reds and golds.
Past them stand eucalypt belts
and remnant bush creeps,
shadowy like an old overcoat.

Behind the wooden house, a hill
deflects winds that buffet
like rampant children.
In its shadow we settle
like autumn lambs between
mothers' legs, protected, nurtured.

Lake Wendouree

Ballarat, Victoria

The lake relaxes into its shape
as if into its favourite armchair,
replete now despite the times of drought
when its muddy bottom spat dust
and the reeds feigned death.
They returned, though, like pestering flies—
the miracle of life.

Rain has started. The distant side of the lake
is obscured but the daily walkers are undeterred
and blinkered like racehorses. Some women hurry—
dampness threatens to turn coiffed hair unruly.

Drops frost the surface of the water
which, only minutes ago, reflected
the colours of the trees, still emerald
despite the season. Pock-marked now,
the lake spreads grey-white like the sky
that presses in. Any warmth of the day
captured in our skin has been breezed away.

The lake belies its urban setting, ignores
traffic noise and the buzz of recess.
Interred in earth, conscious of its own world,
its bones are fleshed with peace.

Road trip to the Snowy Mountains - April

1. Mathoura, New South Wales

The sky is big. It presses on the horizon,
forcing it into the ground. Overcast, grey shapes hang and shift.
Shelter belts huddle, low and dark against
yellow ground. It gets no drier than now.
The break is yet to come.

2. Howlong, New South Wales

Hump-back foothills hunch to warn us
that roads will rise. The sky is held between their hands.
Shadows flood as the sun lowers—
there is no lingering twilight in this country.
Night comes before its time.

3. Corryong, Victoria

The sky is compressed by mountains
grown from valleys running like dry rivers.
Corryong stakes a claim on the flat ground
like a peg holding earth to earth.
Crisp air makes the coffee comforting.

4. Kiandra, New South Wales

Mere pieces of sky peek through eucalypts
leaning together to whisper secrets.
Burnt branches wrapped in furs
and feather boas of new growth, stark against black,
make patterns against the clouds.

5. Top of the Range, New South Wales

Trees diminished, reduced to shrubs,
concede and allow plains to bleed out.
The sky falls and mist is among us.
Heavy air slows the world with white darkness.
We watch for lights of oncoming traffic.

Morning notes

Brunswick, Victoria

It's dark in Brunswick this morning—
already past seven and barely a lightening of the sky
beyond the glow of streetlights still diligent
in their duty. The traffic is waking,
making its grumbly, first-thing noises,
a monster unhappy to be up on a Saturday.
The wind has been working all night. It finishes
its shift with a flourish. The fig tree silhouetted
against the coming sky bends in welcome.
I drink a Nescafé.
The kitchen light is bright,
a lonely warmth against the world's blue-cool.
I'm glad to see the day. I've slept enough.
I let the others doze but the kettle is noisy—
like the traffic
but hopeful.

Pirates Bay

Tasmania

I see a skinny beach, a little around from Eaglehawk Neck, that sports a tiny row of dunes, higher than it is deep, curling around the piece of coastline like a comforting arm. It forms an amphitheatre and I sit in the middle of the audience and look over Pirates Bay to the Tasman Sea. If I could see far enough, the southern mountains of New Zealand would rise into view. The earth curves, however, and human eyes are sadly limited.

The water eats at the slope, foam scurrying up the wet, thieving illicit grains and running away like a taunting sibling. It will return the sand in time. The shape of the land amplifies the sound of waves so the booming and hushing belies their modest size. I close my eyes and the noise moves from side to side as if someone is playing with the settings—left, to the right, left again.

The sand, fine-grained and white, blows onto my jeans and sticks to my jumper when I lie back. It cradles my head and shifts under my wriggling shoulders until I feel I could stay here forever. The cool breeze comes off a sea yet to warm from winter, but the sun is cosy. For me, prostrate, they are perfectly balanced. The sparse seaweed is free from rubbish. The currents must be kind.

There is no-one here apart from my friend who has wandered off photographing—the water, the few boats nearer the point and the plant life are rough and beautiful. A sign says Little Penguins breed nearby. Dogs love to exercise here. There is tension.

We climb the dozen steps to our car parked beside Blowhole Road. Two gulls hang as if suspended from either end of a stick turning in the wind. They see us off, ready to reclaim the beach as their own. They have been most generous to share.

Canberra Glimpses

The lake is crumpled today,
teased by the breeze, a testing sibling.
We drive on a causeway,
straight moment between circles.
We are not lost. Exploring.
Public buildings pull back from the street—
brick and stone blocks where work hides.
The Gallery's treasures, though,
are on display, like grandma's dolls
for us to play with.
In suburbs, empty houses like blinded eyes
grow grass rank and falling.
Next-door pride looks askance,
polishes itself a little harder.
Patches of bush prowl roadsides—
swirls of boysenberry in an ice-cream cup.
Untended they thicken, a rusty cancer
threatening to cleave the city.

V. Too Much Time

After the birth

After the birth
someone hands you a shape,
places it in arms
unused to duty.

Someone takes away the blood
and fibrous masses
that once sustained life
and you are alone for a moment
with newness.

Unseeing eyes search your face
already knowing you.
Tiny baby mouth nuzzles for first food.
Someone helps. It is unfamiliar,
strange, too close.

Someone takes your child for an eternity.
They bring her back washed and smooth,
wrapped
and real.

Relapse

Despair leaves craters in the crèma.
The flower design is spoiled.
A drop sneaks into the black saucer,
a receptacle for sadness.

This morning is worse than yesterday.
Echoes of past anguish whisper—she remembers
hopelessness, fear, her chest crushing
like blackbirds' eggs.

It is familiar, old shoes worn to her shape.
Almost warm. Almost comforting.
A tantalising voice
with a soft blanket to suffer under.

The work of living is a pitted goat track
of clambering and stumbling.
Exhausted already, she orders another coffee—
nothing to be gained from abstinence—
and a piece of carrot cake as breakfast.

Introversion

The corn flowers are hidden. Dusty blue and soft,
they need not retire. They have a right
to the noise of gerberas, to fanfare,
to a place of esteem where flowers go—
the mantlepiece, the centre
of a white linen tablecloth pressed smooth.
Cornflowers deserve, in their purple-grey work clothes,
a seat where petals catch the light
and tiny stamen-shadows dapple sunlit parts.
The cornflowers are hidden as I am hidden.
With quiet strength, we call out.

Balloons that aren't for parties

Loneliness inflates like a party balloon,
pushes ends of the day apart
making the in-between thin.
Loneliness blots out the sun, colour.
Distant figures pass through. Busy busy.
Rush rush. Crumbs of conversation drop.
I swoop, scavenge, gulp like one starved.
Too much myself pools
and spills on the carpet.
It dries before anyone sees
but leaves a mark, a murky tideline
reminding me there is a tomorrow
with a yet-again morning.

Bravado

Bravado likes to play hide and seek—
hiding you, seeking the stage.
Bravado drags you, chirping,
into sky diving and drinking games.

Bravado's suit is too big for your body
but covers you when you are naked.
Bravado speaks loudly, a ventriloquist's doll
for your whispers.

Bravado nicks off sometimes,
can't be bothered,
leaves you alone, perched in a tree,
unsure of how to get down.

Clutter

Clutter sprawls, lounges thickly on your couch,
refuses to move when you ask it nicely.
It reclines on your surfaces and says you're in too deep.
Clutter smirks at your attempts to find the carpet
where it's left hair and sticky plates.
Clutter is every-coloured. It smells like failure.
Clutter taps your ankle with a chipped ornament
and lies on your chest when you fall.
It holds you under with heavy papers.
Clutter wears all your clothes, screws up your socks
and leaves one shoe by the bed.
It fears nothing, openly grows in the middle of the room.
Clutter whispers *'give up'* in your ear.

At Water's Edge

In an eddy off Collins Street,
safe from the rapids of lunchtime,
a young couple talk,
lost from the stream of Thursday,
treading water with each other.

She cries. Sinks.
Long fingers with painted nails droop
disconsolate on her short, black skirt.
He strokes her neck,
whispers, *I'm sorry*
to the space between them,

wades in the flood of pain
that rises like the water
from the fountain opposite.

Drenched by shadows of buildings
that have lasted through time
they navigate the end
of something that has not.

Notifications

They sell stickers in the Post Office that say
'FRAGILE'.
I was pleasantly surprised.
What a thoughtful thing,
providing such a useful item
for those like me
who feel that way at times.
I did think the chemist may be
a better place to stock them,
with other health-related products,
but was gratified to know
where to go when I needed one.
I may enquire
whether their range extends to
'PREPARED'
or even 'HOPEFUL'.

Too much time

The clock has no hands—an eyeless face.
Time is unmeasured.
-

There is too much,
like aged skin no longer required.
-

-

It swamps, drowns.
It weighs on my body
slumped like yesterday's laundry.
-

-

-

Time floods. I am a glass under a firehose.
Gushing hours inundate. I wade.
-

-

-

-

My socks, my clothes are sodden.
Time rises. I am submerged, subsumed.
My wet hair drifts like weed on its tide.
-

-

-

-

-

Too much time—acres broad and deserted,
empty like days.

VI. Art Should

Shy dogs

Like oil, poems are slippery. I crouch and smile,
click my fingers and call encouragingly
as if to a shy dog, but poems are shyer.
We don't even reach discourse; they curve away,
mercury-fluid, uncatchable. I know they're there;
they reflect light—moons out of reach—
and bend gravity like planets.

They guard secret hearts
with dark cloaks that slide like satin,
ripple out of your hands when you try to grasp.
So, play at not caring. Play at moving on
and becoming a painter. Poems,
for all their reticence, don't like being left behind.
Like the shy dog running after a car,
a poem will arrive, innocent, as if it were simply delayed.

Art should

after Ars Poetica by Archibald MacLeish

Art should give voice to the moment
that strikes like a bird wing then soars away,
should call attention to a single thought that flits and flees,
should trap a feeling in line and shade.

Art should tingle like a touch,
describe a glorious instant with marks,
bring the unnoticed notice, like a sign with an arrow:
'Here is human truth.'

Art should dance deftly with feet that float
above a timber floor, should capture and release
like a fish destined to live
or a butterfly escaped from its hiding.

Art should take the detritus of our lives—
dust, hairs, leaf litter blown to the gutters—
polish it to beauty, bring back
the grains of sand we lost.

Laura's Mother the Poet

I don't like to clean the house
so words bank up in the corners
and dangle from daddy-long-legs' webs.
Ideas rumble with biscuit bits
and images collect on my windowsill
with flies and parts of moth wings.

I don't enjoy cooking.
Rhythms stir the rice
and mumbled lines carve the onions
into crooked pieces. When the meal is ready
I write and leave the casserole to dry.

I tell Laura stories at bedtime:
the vibrant adventures
of Bill, the bohemian headmaster,
and Margot, the one-legged explorer.
The sheets need changing
but the seeds for her dreams are well sown.

Musings on a bottle

It is a blue bottle, a small bottle two inches high
with patterned sides, forged from liquid.
It is a stoppered bottle that once held bottled things
like perfume. A bottle to carry in a bag
with handkerchiefs and gloves.
A glass bottle, old, precious now.
Valuable bottles are rare,
not like bottles in the recycling.
It is a beautiful bottle, refracting light,
cerulean bottle shadow on its far side.
Bottle, bottle, bottle, compact word beating like a heart.
Brittle, like a bottle, a small blue bottle,
stoppered, patterned, two inches high, bottle.

When I die

When I die, scrape together my paintings
and hang them on any old wall.
Give them away. Let people take what they like.
Sow seeds of new art, planting with hands
that held mine and their painty skin.

When I die, seek out the watercolourists,
the sketchers, the teachers,
and let them browse through boxes,
have what materials they love.
I will be remembered
in a child's sun or a seascape.

When I die, clean out my studio,
return it to a room where people dine together.
Display a painting if you like, but open the windows
and let in some rain.

Biography

Kirsten Johnston is a poet from regional South Australia. She writes to give the small moments of life a voice—to capture fleeting instances and impressions and bring to light the tiny joys, anomalies and beauties that are often missed. The other half of Kirsten's creative life is her work as a visual artist in which she paints large-scale abstract pieces for exhibition and sale, often inspired, like her poetry, by small treasures within our existence.

Publishing/awards:

'Going Home from Robe', *Tamba*, No 70, June 2022

'Autumn Progeny', *Friendly Street Reader 47*, 2023

'Vintage', *Milang Community News*, June 2022

'Scrabbling At the Grape', Café, *Anthology of Writing and Images*, ed Megan Surmon and Simon Jackson, 1999

'Canonisation of St Mary, *Poetrix*, Issue 37, November 2011

'Sunflowers', *Muse*, No 188, September 1999

'Old Merv', *Tamba*, Spring/Summer, 2010

'Cold', *Tamba*, No 70, June 2022

'Rain', *Poetrix*, Issue 37, November 2011

'Lake Wendouree', Highly Commended, Laura Literary Awards, 2022

'Road Trip to the Snowy Mountains – April', *Friendly Street Reader 47*, 2023

'At Water's Edge', Second Place, Logan City Writing Awards, 2009

'Notifications', *Tamba*, Spring/Summer, 2010

'Shy Dogs', *4W* thirty three, Nov 2022

'Laura's Mother the Poet', *Muse*, No 192, February 2000